W9-AAM-597

SPACE MISSIONS™

The Mercury 6 Mission

The First American Astronaut to Orbit Earth

Helen Zelon

The Rosen Publishing Group's
PowerKids Press™
New York

For Michael Zelon, space communications pioneer, who made his dreams a reality

Published in 2002 by The Rosen Publishing Group, Inc.
29 East 21st Street, New York, NY 10010

First Edition

Book Design: Michael de Guzman
Project Editors: Jennifer Landau, Jennifer Quasha, Jason Moring

Photo credits: p. 4 © Photri-Microstock (Sputnik), © Archive Photos (Y. Gagarin), © Bettmann/CORBIS (Y. Gagarin in space suit); p. 7 © Photri-Microstock; p. 8 © Bettmann/CORBIS; p. 9 Courtesy of NASA/JPL/California Institute of Technology; p. 11 Digital image © 1996 CORBIS; p. 12 Courtesy of NASA/JPL/California Institute of Technology; pp. 15, 20 © Bettmann/CORBIS; pp. 16, 18 Courtesy of NASA/JPL/California Institute of Technology; p. 19 Courtesy of NASA/JPL/California Institute of Technology (top left, bottom left, bottom right), © Photri-Microstock (top right).

Zelon, Helen.
The Mercury 6 mission: the first American astronaut to orbit Earth/
Helen Zelon.—1st ed.
p. cm. — (Space missions)
Includes index.
ISBN 0-8239-5770-5 (library binding)
1. Project Mercury (U.S.)—Juvenile literature. 2. Friendship 7 (Spacecraft)—Juvenile literature. 3. Glenn, John, 1921—Juvenile literature. 4. Project Mercury (U.S.) [1. Glenn, John, 1921– 2. Astronauts.] I. Title. II. Series.
TL789.8.U6 M549 2002
629.45'4'0973—dc21

00-012311

Manufactured in the United States of America

Contents

MERCURY 6
Friendship
GLENN

The Space Race

MERCURY 6 Friendship 7 GLENN

In 1903, Orville Wright flew the first airplane. Orville Wright's first flight lasted for 12 seconds. By the 1950s, the United States and the Soviet Union had developed powerful rockets that would allow people to fly outside of Earth's **atmosphere**. These countries competed to see which would be the first to explore outer space. The Soviets kept their space program a secret. They surprised the world twice. In 1957, they launched *Sputnik*, the first **satellite** in space. In 1961, a **cosmonaut** named Yuri Gagarin became the first man in space. Gagarin **orbited** Earth once in a flight that lasted for 108 minutes. The Soviets' victories made the Americans even more determined to win what was called the "space race."

← *The large photo shows a model of* Sputnik. *The photographs below show the Soviet cosmonaut Gagarin.*

Friendship 7

America's first space program was called Project Mercury. The seven astronauts chosen for the program were experienced military **test pilots.** They were called the Mercury 7. Only one of the team of astronauts took part in each mission. The astronaut chosen for a mission named his **space capsule**. All of the names ended in "7" for the seven astronauts on the Mercury team.

On May 5, 1961, Alan Shepard Jr. became the first American **launched** into space. This was an important first step for America's space program. The next step was to have an American astronaut orbit Earth. John Herschel Glenn Jr. was the astronaut chosen for the Mercury 6 mission. Glenn named his space capsule *Friendship 7*.

The space suits worn by the seven Mercury 7 astronauts let them travel to space safely. →

MERCURY 6
Friendship
7
GLENN

Godspeed, John Glenn

Before daylight on February 20, 1962, John Glenn woke up, showered, and ate a breakfast of steak, scrambled eggs, toast, orange juice, and coffee. It was a very important day in Glenn's life. It was the day of the Mercury 6 launch. By dawn, Glenn had dressed in his 20-pound (9.1-kg) space suit. Getting into the space capsule was a snug fit. Engineers and scientists at **Mission Control** would guide Glenn's journey from the ground. John Glenn sat inside the *Friendship 7* capsule at the tip of a 90-foot (27.4-m) rocket. "Godspeed, John Glenn," said astronaut Scott Carpenter, speaking to him from Mission Control. At 9:47 A.M., *Friendship 7* roared into the sky.

There was so little room in the space capsule that Glenn's helmet was only 18 inches (46 cm) from the instrument panels.

Orbiting the Earth

Five minutes after liftoff on February 20, 1962, *Friendship 7* entered its orbital path, the path it would take around Earth. Glenn would travel around the world three times. Each orbit was 25,300 miles (41,000 km) and took only 88 minutes. Engineers tracked *Friendship 7* as it made its way across the Atlantic Ocean, Africa, the Indian Ocean, and Australia. Although it was midnight in Australia, the lights in the cities of Perth and Rockingham were left on to greet Glenn as he flew above.

During his first sunrise in space, Glenn was shocked to see thousands of sparkling bits swirling around the capsule window. The bits were frost crystals reflecting the sunlight. This phenomenon was named the Glenn effect after its discoverer.

John Glenn kept his helmet on in orbit. From space, Glenn saw an amazing sunrise (middle). *Glenn also had a great view of Earth from inside* Friendship 7.

MERCURY 6
Friendship 7
GLENN

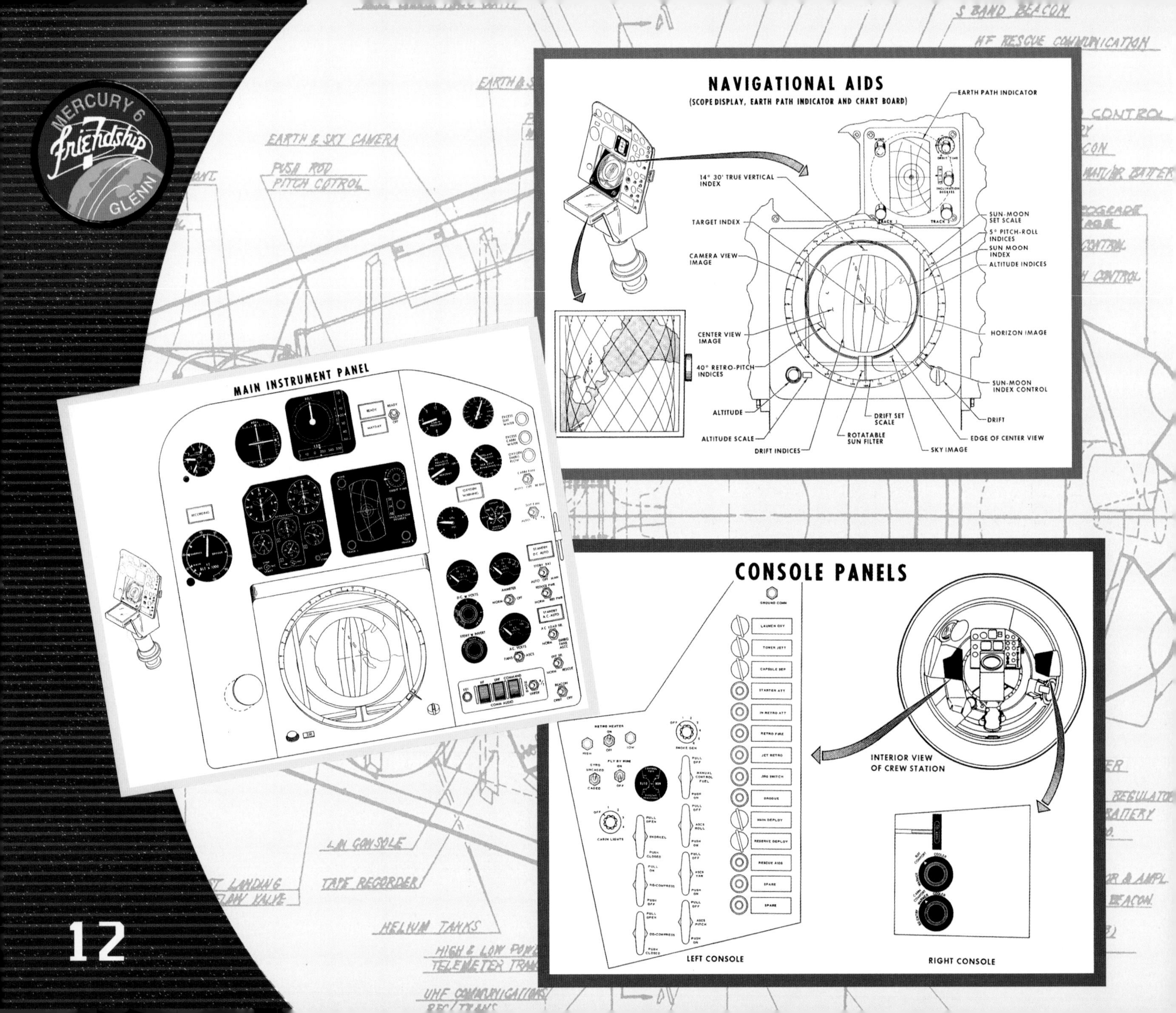
MERCURY 6
Friendship
GLENN
NAVIGATIONAL AIDS
(SCOPE DISPLAY, EARTH PATH INDICATOR AND CHART BOARD)
EARTH PATH INDICATOR
14° 30' TRUE VERTICAL INDEX
TARGET INDEX
CAMERA VIEW IMAGE
CENTER VIEW IMAGE
40° RETRO-PITCH INDICES
ALTITUDE
ALTITUDE SCALE
DRIFT INDICES
ROTATABLE SUN FILTER
DRIFT SET SCALE
SKY IMAGE
EDGE OF CENTER VIEW
DRIFT
SUN-MOON INDEX CONTROL
HORIZON IMAGE
ALTITUDE INDICES
SUN MOON INDEX
5° PITCH-ROLL INDICES
SUN-MOON SET SCALE
MAIN INSTRUMENT PANEL
CONSOLE PANELS
INTERIOR VIEW OF CREW STATION
LEFT CONSOLE
RIGHT CONSOLE
EARTH & SKY CAMERA
PUSH ROD PITCH CONTROL
TAPE RECORDER
HELIUM TANKS
S BAND BEACON

Taking Control

During Glenn's second orbit around Earth, the *Friendship 7* capsule began tilting too far to the right. It was straying from its planned orbital path. Automatic equipment on the spacecraft didn't fix the problem, so Glenn fired small rockets on the sides of the spacecraft. The rockets helped him steer the capsule and keep it on course. The extra rocket blasts used valuable fuel, but Glenn had to keep the capsule in orbit.

John Glenn was the first American astronaut to eat in space. An hour and four minutes into his flight, he squeezed applesauce into his mouth through a tube. The tube was used because there are no effects of **gravity** in space. A blob of applesauce would have floated off into the space capsule's cabin if Glenn had tried to use a spoon.

← *Control panels like these gave John Glenn the information he needed to fly* Friendship 7 *around the globe.*

MERCURY 6
Friendship 7
GLENN

Danger in Space

As John Glenn continued his flight on February 20, 1962, engineers on the ground worried about his safety. A signal at Mission Control showed that the landing bag on *Friendship 7* might be loose. The landing bag cushions the capsule's fall into the ocean at the end of a mission. It also holds the **heat shield** in place. The heat shield is the only thing that keeps an astronaut from burning up as his capsule reenters Earth's atmosphere.

Three retrorockets held the landing bag and heat shield in place. Retrorockets, held in place by a retropack, are used to slow down a spacecraft or change its direction. Mission Control scientists decided to leave on the retropack for as long as possible. They hoped that the retropack would hold the heat shield in place, as well.

If John Glenn's heat shield had come loose, he would have been unprotected from the 3,000-degree Fahrenheit (1,648.9-degree C.) heat when he came back into Earth's atmosphere.

MERCURY 6
Friendship
GLENN

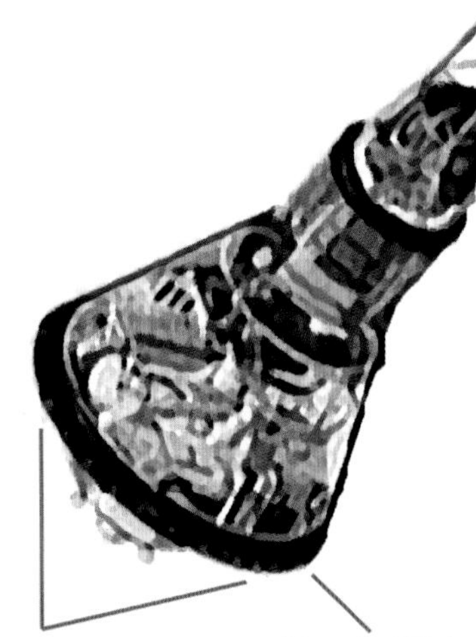
Retrograde
Package
Heat Shield

Holding onto the Heat Shield

As John Glenn orbited Earth for the last time, Mission Control told him about the problem with *Friendship 7's* heat shield. Glenn didn't panic. He prepared to reenter Earth's atmosphere. Scientists believed that the straps that held the capsule's retropack also would hold the heat shield in place. Although the straps would burn during **reentry**, the heat shield would stay in place to keep the capsule from burning. When a space capsule reenters Earth's atmosphere, it goes through a fiery area and the astronaut cannot speak to Mission Control. When *Friendship 7* did lose contact, no one knew if it would survive. Glenn saw flaming metal fly by his window. He thought that the heat shield was falling away from the capsule. The *Friendship 7* began to rock and it ran out of fuel. For 51 seconds, *Friendship 7* was in freefall.

← *Clockwise from top left: the heat shield, Mission Control, Glenn parachutes toward reentry, and retropack and heat shield.*

A Safe Landing

Nearly five hours after its launch, *Friendship 7* fell toward Earth. John Glenn struggled to release the parachute that would slow the capsule's drop into the ocean. Just as he reached up, the chute opened.

The capsule floated down through the clouds. The U.S. **destroyer** *Noa* spotted it and quickly steamed over to pick up Glenn and his capsule. "It was hot in there," Glenn said to the sailors on the *Noa*. The sailors celebrated Glenn's successful mission by painting his footsteps

This pin was worn by many proud Americans upon John Glenn's return.

on the deck. A large burned area on the *Friendship 7* capsule was proof that the heat shield had held and had protected Glenn's return to Earth.

The Friendship 7 *is being loaded on* Noa.

The capsule holding Glenn is lifted out of the water.

Glenn is looking at the capsule after his rescue.

Friendship 7 *is being inspected by rescue crew.*

A Hero's Welcome

On February 26, 1962, more than 250,000 people lined the rainy, cold streets of Washington, D.C., to see John Glenn. Newspapers from all over the world reported on Glenn's 20-minute speech to **Congress**. In New York City, March 1 was renamed John Glenn Day. Millions stood in freezing temperatures to be part of the city's **ticker tape** parade, which honored all seven of the Mercury 6 astronauts. Two days later, in Glenn's hometown of New Concord, Ohio, more than 75,000 people turned out to welcome him.

The *Friendship 7* capsule made another trip around the world. This time it was safely on the ground, on a traveling display to 17 countries and the American state of Hawaii. On the first anniversary of the Mercury 6 mission, the capsule was on view in Washington, D.C., where it still can be seen today.

← *John Glenn rides with his wife and Vice-President Lyndon B. Johnson in a parade to celebrate his safe return from space.*

Back in Space

In the years after the Mercury 6 mission, Glenn worked with the space program and in business. Glenn also served four six-year terms in the U.S. Senate as a senator from Ohio.

John Glenn returned to space thirty-six years after the Mercury 6 mission. He was 77 years old when he served as **payload specialist** on the Space Shuttle mission STS-95. As part of the STS-95 team, Glenn completed 134 orbits and logged more than 3.6 million miles (5.8 million km) in space. This was far longer and far greater than his 3-orbit, 75,679-mile (121,794-km) solo journey during the Mercury 6 mission in 1962. However, without his **pioneer** flight the American space program might not have grown to be the leader it is today.

Glossary

atmosphere (AT-muh-sfeer) The layer of gases that surrounds an object in space. On Earth, this layer is air.

Congress (KON-gres) The part of the U.S. government that makes laws and is made up of the House of Representatives and the Senate.

cosmonaut (KOZ-moh-not) A Russian astronaut.

destroyer (dih-STROY-ur) Fast warship armed with guns, missiles, and torpedoes.

gravity (GRA-vih-tee) The natural force that causes objects to move or tend to move toward the center of Earth.

heat shield (HEET SHEELD) A shield that protects a spacecraft from burning up as it returns to Earth.

launched (LAWNCHD) Pushed out or put into the air.

Mission Control (MISH-shun kun-TROHL) A group of scientists that controls a space mission from the ground.

orbited (OR-bih-tid) When one body takes a path around another, usually larger, body.

payload specialist (PAY-lohd SPEH-shuh-list) Scientist who conducts experiments and maneuvers on a space mission.

pioneer (py-uh-NEER) First.

reentry (ree-EN-tree) Returning to Earth's atmosphere from space.

satellite (SA-til-eyet) A human-made or natural object that orbits another body. The moon is Earth's natural satellite.

space capsule (SPAYS KAP-sul) Spacecraft.

test pilots (TEST PY-litz) People who are trained to fly airplanes and test how well the planes work.

ticker tape (TIK-er TAYP) Thin pieces of paper that people throw out of windows during parades.

Index

Web Sites

To find out more about the Mercury 6 mission and spaceflight, check out these Web sites:

http://spaceflight.nasa.gov

http://www.jsc.nasa.gov